POETRY WILL ALWAYS BE A PART OF OUR LIVES.

Copyright © 2024 by Richard Jacks

All rights reserved. No part of this book may be reproduced in any manner whatsoever without written permission except in the case of brief quotations embodied in critical articles and reviews.

First Printing, 2024

Poetry Will Always Be A Part Of Our Lives.

Richard Jacks

BTP Publishing

Contents

Words from the Author ix

Afraid But Not Afraid	1
If Love Is A Beautiful Thing...	2
If Love Comes Your Way...	4
What Was Your Age...	6
Princess Diana, We Love You	8
Queen Elizabeth II	10
Living And Love	11
Mistakes	13
Loneliness	14
My Sanctuary	15
Pretending To Care	16
My Neighborhood	17
Coming And Going	18
Shopping Spree	19

Wish List	20
Drugs	21
Money	22
Sunny	23
My Own Car	24
Trapped	25
Party Prep	26
Party Time	27
Church Fashion Show	28
Raining	29
Dinner	30
Sunshine	31
After Party	32
School Work	33
My Thoughts	34
Mad Woman	35
In My Heart	36
Infatuation	37
My Lesson	38
Change My Heart	39
Why?	40

Grocery List	41
I Miss You	43
Cleaning Day	44
Library Blues	45
People Around Town	46
The Fall	47
Talk About It	48
Last Words Of A Friend	49
Life Chances	51
Snack Shop	52
You Are Beautiful...	54
When Is The Best Time...	55
I Remember...	56
Can We Live...	57
There Are People...	58
One Day I Was In A Store	59
You Know A Neighbor	60
When A Princess	61
There Is A Woman	62
I Know A Lady	63
Lady	64

Man	65
Your Face Is Beautiful	66
I Love You	67
When I See You	68
A Good Neighbor's Love	69
I Love When You Love Me Baby	71
I Love To See Your Light Shine	73
The Love Of Christmas	75
Hello Weekend	77

It is a great day for writing,
and it happens that way.
I feel that something good comes out of it.
A great feeling that you can gather your
thoughts together and transform your
mind into a way that everyone can enjoy.
Since I have been writing, I have enjoyed myself,
showing people what I have come up with and
share the gift of writing that God has instilled in
me. It amazes me when I sit down to rest, and a
word or two would come to mind. I instantly will
jot it down until I am ready to polish it, and put it
in the manner it should go. When you write think
about good things, and good things will come.
You might not understand it then but the words
will start flowing in your mind when you least
expect it to. So, surround yourself with love, and
keep a notepad and pencil close by. Nevertheless,
keep it on your mind so that you can share it with
others, Thanks to all who paved the way for me.

-Richard Jacks, Author

Afraid But Not Afraid

I'm not afraid to die,
because I know that there's
a great reward beyond the sky.

I was born alone,
But had people around me that were great.

I'm not afraid to die,
But I am afraid to die
not knowing what true love
feels like.

If Love Is A Beautiful Thing...

If love is a beautiful thing

If love is a beautiful thing,
Why can't most people
seem to understand?

What are three greatest gifts

What are three greatest gifts,
God has given to us?
Wisdom,
Knowledge,
and Understanding.

If you could touch

If you could touch
and feel love,
would it be the same?
No, because love is a feeling,
that we can't explain.

What is the only way

What is the only way,
to make love exciting?
Don't talk about it.

If Love Comes Your Way...

If love comes your way

If love comes your way
would you know?
Yes!
Because,
I've been down that road before.

If love comes from the heart

If love comes from the heart,
where does love go
when it leaves the heart?

Love is so beautiful

Love is so beautiful
if you have it.
If you don't have it,
Love will come around again.

Love is outstanding

Love is outstanding,
Love is great.
Love is deep down in your heart.
No matter what,
Love will remain forever.

What Was Your Age...

What was your age

What was your age,
when did you become old?
I can't remember,
I'm still trying to get there.

There are six senses

There are six senses.
But the only one
commonly never used,
is the six sense.
Common sense.

What is the best way

What is the best way
to gain success?
Fail at first,
maybe the second.
Don't give up,
keep trying,
Success will come.

Princess Diana, We Love You

You were a true princess to all of those around.
But it all came from within and not because you wore a crown.
All of the children admired you.
And we did too.
Princess Di, we love you.

Good luck to your children, your family and friends.
I know they'll miss you too. You always kept them within your heart.
Princess Di, we love you.

Even when you were far away,
I know they loved you so much,
Because you had such a loving touch.
This we know and understand.
Princess Di, we love you.

Everything is so beautiful.
Seems like you are here.
I want everybody to know,
That what we had is gone.
Princess Di, we love you.

Accidents do happen. Indeed they can.
This we know, and understand.
You've visited the poor and disabled.
I wondered how you made time.
You never forgot people in a crisis.
Princess Di, we love you.

You've worked for charities and it's a great cause.
We all stood up and gave you a standing applause. I thought that was very loving and kind.
We all miss you and I know everything will be alright.
Princess Di, we love you.

Queen Elizabeth II

I would like to write a poem if I can,
I think your answer will be go ahead, and when you are
ready to write in a beautiful form, I know you can.
So, as I start, you are a Queen in and out, the life you
carry around with you explains it all.

70 years as the Queen in your life.
You were always here when it was time to appear, your
light shines far and near.
You were a true Queen.

Living And Love

My song is living.
My song is Love.
I hope my song
will be loved by everyone.
This is what I'll say,
this is what I'll do.
I'll keep on loving you
I'll always love you.
I always will.
What is the reason,
why I cant love you still?
Sweetheart, I love you.
I know you love me.
I'm singing my love song
just for you.
Living is the answer
Love is the reason why.
I'll always love you
and that's no lie.
I'm singing my song,
I'm singing my song just for you.

This is my story.
This is my song
and learned right from wrong.
I'm singing my song.
I hope my song
will be loved by everyone
I'm singing my song,
I'm singing my song just for you.
Living, and so much
in love

Mistakes

We all make mistakes,
 that we have to learn from.
Some of which,
we learn immediately
after the lesson was taught.
Others come later
and some of which,
with a price,
they are bought.

Loneliness

Loneliness has its ups and downs.
There's no one to bother you,
when you're busy relaxing
or reading a good book.
The down side of it is,
when you have good news,
there's no one to share it with.
When you cry,
who is there to dry your tears?
Loneliness is my
greatest fear.

My Sanctuary

My bedroom is my sanctuary.
I feel safe and secure
in my bedroom.
When I am alone,
my entire home
is my safe haven.
But when I share my space,
with someone else,
my bedroom is my sacred
place.

Pretending To Care

I'm pretending to care,
in fact, I don't care at all.
All of the abuse I had to endure,
If God is not involved.
From pain,
there is no careT
I pretend to care,
only to make myself look good.
Don't get it twisted or misunderstood.
I only pretend to care,
because it looks good
in the public eye.
But really, I don't care.
When everyone is gone,
I just sit back and cry.
I tried so hard
pretending not to care.
That's all I did.

My Neighborhood

My neighborhood seems as though its for
people who are settled.
It's just a thought, and I'm not looking for a silver medal.
If there's someone around that's my age,
they are married with children.
A baby on board is not what I'm feeling.
Sometimes, I want to get away from the neighborhood,
but not for too long.
I'm proud of my neighborhood.
I call it home.

Coming And Going

Sometimes I don't know if I'm coming or going.
Confusion is something I'm not afraid of showing.
Sometimes I don't know if I'm coming or going.
So many things are going on around me that,
I don't know what I want or where I want to be.

Shopping Spree

I want to go on a shopping spree.
It's been a long time since, I spent lots of money.
I would like to fill my drawers with lots of boxer briefs,
these I could never have too many of.
I would like to fill my closet with jogging suits.
That would look good on me.
I would like put on some shades to block the sun from my eyes.
Yes, having two pairs, I'm that guy!
Add snake skin boots, will make the ladies go wild!
I'm that guy to go out in style.
Of course, in good health is what I want to be.
Shopping sprees may have me exhausted at the end of the day,
but it's what I need after I get paid.

Wish List

I have a wish list, yes I do!
I have a wish list. How about you?
I am looking through a catalog and there's a lot to see.
There's a camera that snaps still shots,
and videos too.
I'm glad that it comes in the color of blue.
A fifteen inch flat screen television would do just fine.
A bistro dinette set would be nice to dine,
for those moments when guest are over.
I will get a bottle of wine to drink off of the wine rack
don't drink too much! It will cause a hangover.
A wine clock hanging over the new dinette set
would look good.
The concept would be well understood.
There is a four piece lamp set, will go
well in the living room.
I am saving up to buy all of those things, real soon!

Drugs

Drugs are a powerful thing.
It causes mood swings.
Drugs are mind-altering,
it makes you do strange things.
When the drug wears off, the person becomes sober.
Consequences may have just begun.
It just might not be over.

Money

Money is the root of all evil,
but it's not always true.
Let me have some and I will show you.
I have made a wish list to accomplish one day.
If I had some money.
I would buy all of the things on the wish list.
Then the wish list would go away.

Sunny

Its a sunny day outside.
The rain is over for now,
and the sun is shining.
It is scorching hot, and I need to be in a pool of
water to cool me off.
Come all, sons and daughters!

My Own Car

I need my own car!
I'm tired of sitting around the house with nothing to do.
If I had a car, riding around is what I would do.
Give me the chance to purchase a car, and I will show you.
Walking around is good exercise,
but having a car is well off, I can't deny.
I need a car, I really do.
I need a car, to do the things I want to do.

Trapped

Some people put blame on others for who
they have become.
Only to find themselves trapped in their excuses.
Your eyes will never open if you
are afraid to look at the bigger picture.
Which is your situation.
At times, I feel trapped inside a box and
I want to get out.
I don't know how or what's the next step.
It is like a baby standing up, balancing themselves.
Moving their feet to take a step in walking, but
they need some encouragement.
They need some help.
I can't be trapped no longer.
I need to escape and break free.

Party Prep

Its time to prep the food for the party.
It will be good, so don't be tardy.
There will be some barbeque chicken.
Take one bite, and you're finger lickin.
Put some potato salad on your plate,
for some baked beans save some space.
All of this food has to cook for perfection.
I don't want to get anyone sick, or cause an infection.

Party Time

It's party time!
Time to celebrate.
Cook some food, pour up some drinks.
Its party time, who cares what you think?
Turn on the music, because I want to groove.
Good music makes me move.
Fix me a plate,
because when I am done,
I want a slice of cake.
It's party time, party time, party time!

Church Fashion Show

It seems like when I go to church
with a large congregation,
it's nothing but a fashion show.
What happened to preachers that
had a desire to save souls?
They treat the collection plates like a pot of gold .
Church is like a fashion show.
If you make enough money,
you can sit on the front row,
They preach prosperity and good health, but
what about the hell that folks raise during the week?
Once they die and their soul isn't right,
they won't like hells heat.
Clean clothes don't mean a thing
when your heart is dirty.
Heaven is my goal, and I want to be worthy.

Raining

It is raining, and the sun is not out.
It is raining, and I have nothing to shout about.
If the rain doesn't stop today...
I don't know what I will do for my birthday.

Dinner

Is it dinner time? I don't know.
I need to eat, before my stomach groans.
I sometimes eat breakfast, and lunch too .
If I miss dinner, a snack will do.
Dinner is what I prepare!
Look into my pots if you dare!

Sunshine

The sun is out and there is sunshine.
The sun is so hot,
on the side walk you can fry an egg on the spot.
Make sure you have a bottle of water to stay hydrated.
Keep your bottles of water filled.
To dehydrate will make your body feel ill.
There is a lot of sunshine on the earth.
The grass is growing,
and in the air the trees are blowing.

After Party

I had a good time at my party.
I wanted to give one before I was forty.
I had music and alcohol too.
It's my party and I would have cried,
if that was what I wanted to do.
There was barbeque chicken
and spaghetti with cheese.
They had potato salad on the side,
and everyone was pleased.
After we were full,
we hit the dance floor.
We wanted to party all night,
but I couldn't take no more.

School Work

I have so much homework to do,
that I am overwhelmed.
 I am so exhausted,
can't you tell?
You would think I got it all straight,
being that it's only three days late.
Homework, please slow down.
I am trying to keep my sanity,
but these instructions are
getting the best of me.
When I am done,
I could rest.
Next semester,
I will do my best

My Thoughts

Some people hate to see me independent,
and self-sufficient.
Nothing is going to stop me
or block me from reaching my goals.
Striving for excellence never gets old.
Right now,
I might be at the bottom,
striving to reach the top.
However long it takes me to get there,
I am on my way.
Sometimes I have to cry,
not knowing there will ever be a brighter day.
Troubles always come my way.

Mad Woman

You tell me that you care about me,
but I don't see it.
You say that you're my man,
but it seems like you don't want to be it.
Don't tell me all of those lies just to make you look good.
Because if you don't hold to your word,
I will make you wish you would.
I don't have time for you to sell me any dreams.
When I go to sleep,
I can get them for free.
I am mad at you.
Why be,
when you started out telling me the truth?
The signs were there, giving me all types of signals.
I didn't care, but stayed around and mingled.
At the end, I still have my dignity.
On myself, there is no pity.

In My Heart

I don't know what to do in this situation.
In the past, I was just used to being patient.
I was told that I couldn't be loved like I want to be,
because the person got all of the love
that was before me, I beg to differ.
I'm hypnotizing like a stripper.
Just give me a chance to prove to you
that you will be in love with me boo.
You try and guard your heart,
but the very moment you slip up,
Cupid hits it with a dart.
Pretty soon you will be mine.
Stop, and take a look at the signs.

Infatuation

I rather live and be alone than live unhappy.
The one that you think you are in love with,
you find that it's just infatuation.
It was never love.
Infatuation will have you thinking that it's all about you.
It will have you thinking that man or woman
loves all that they see in you.
They can make you laugh.
Sometimes things get rough.
They will even make you cry.
Infatuation will make you feel that
on him or her,
you can rely.
Infatuation should be just that.
Things need to be left to the imagination.
If we as men and women don't explore the
insides of the infatuation before introducing
ourselves to it,
it could save us from hurt and pain
across the entire nation.

My Lesson

I thought I learned my lesson with
my last relationship.
I guess people don't want to be
faithful no more and this is a trip.
Sometimes they tell the truth.
But most of the time, they tell lies.
When you find out who a person really is,
it makes you want to cry.
God, what is the lesson you are trying to teach me?
Give me the mind to learn.
Open my eyes so that I can see.

Change My Heart

Lord, you wouldn't be God if you changed
my heart from good to bad.
Being good hearted makes me feel so sad.
It seems like I'm always getting used and abused.
Changing my heart from good to bad,
you must refuse.
To shake hands with the devil is no idea of mine.
Me and my heart will do just fine.
I guess I will just ask God to give me strength
to endure this heart ache.
Because the heart you gave me,
you made no mistake.

Why?

Why does happiness have to come with a price?
Just being happy is not at all that nice.
People have always said, "No pain, no gain."
To gain happiness, it starts out with pain.
There is no reason to play the blame game.
Happiness has no certain person to cling to.
Why do we have to go through the
struggle to be happy?
Happiness is the time when you
and your love first met.
Why can't I find happiness?
And so now, I find myself in too deep.

Grocery List

I need to make a grocery list so that I could buy
some food for my house.
I am going to make sure that they
are securely stored.
I am not making groceries for a little mouse.
I got to make groceries,
because I want to eat.
I do not want to starve,
like a man on the streets.
Making groceries may take up some time to do.
When you walk up to the register,
what amount is due?
I put a pack of beans in my basket with some rice too.
That is quite nice.
I pick up a bag of flour,
and a mixture of seasonings.
A bag of potatoes would be pleasing.
Give me this,
and give me that.
I want some eggs,
so I can make some flap jacks.

I can use some bread to make sandwiches
to fill my belly.
Maybe make some peanut better and jelly.
By that time my list is through, I will be so full,
I wouldn't know what to do.

I Miss You

I miss you all of the time.
I miss you,
and you continue to stay on my mind.
When I don't hear from you,
it makes me sad and blue.

I miss you so much,
words can't explain.
I love it when someone mentions your name.
I miss you my love.
When can I see you?
You and I can be alone,
and not have the entire crew.
I miss you baby.
Come on home my sweet lady.

Cleaning Day

The party is over,
and it is time to clean up the mess.
I hate to do it,
because partying is what I do best.
Get a trash bag and pick up
the paper plates and cups.
Do not stop there,
because you have more to clean.
I know that it is tough.
Wash the pots and pans.
Get to cleaning, and use your hands.
Wipe off the counter and the stove.
You might get sweaty,
so you can wash your clothes.
Sweep and mop the floors,
because you are almost done.
I must say that I had a good time.
I had some fun.

Library Blues

I got the library blues.
I don't hear any bad or good news.
I am in here typing on my laptop.
Talking to my friend and his wonderful
ideas that just won't stop.
It is part of the plan, that I am his right hand man.
He is trying to reach his goals.
Can you understand?
This library is so quiet.
That's the way that it is supposed to be.
It is so quiet, you can hear a jumping flea.

People Around Town

The people around town are something.
They don't have any motivation.
They wait on people to give them a helping hand.
Food stamps and welfare checks, that they think are worth one hundred grand.
Those people who work are working to stay alive.
Those who stand on the corners,
it doesn't matter if their mothers cry after seeing them die.
The struggle of people in my town,
is from ignorance that can greatly be found.
A long time ago we were warned.
Being slow to man's plan is greatly charmed.
If you let things stop you from being a success,
all you will have is a big mess.

The Fall

The fall is here, and at first I couldn't tell.
The fall is here, so ring the church bell.
Fall is here and it is time to get our gloves and coats.
Children are in school, so get your lunch boxes and totes.
Soon the holiday season will begin.
It's a time to spend with family and friends.
Laughter and a whole lot of cheer.
When it is cold outside, it makes me want to stay in.
Let's bake some cookies and roast some
marshmallows by the fireplace.
When it is time, we can go outside and play in the snow.
Throwing snowballs and playing chase.

Talk About It

We can sit here and talk about anything.
There is a lot of things that the brain thinks.
Talk about the news or the sports.
Women talk about shopping and shoes.
Staying around the ladies all day,
will give you the blues.
Lets talk about politics,
you know the politicians,
I sometimes cannot get with.
Talk about the preachers and the teacher.
How many times have they greeted us?
Lets talk about the children and how they are raised.
They are having bad attitudes and making bad grades.
There is much more to talk about you see.
There is a lot to talk about, and it's just not for me.

Last Words Of A Friend

Lord I can't get off track with serving you.
You have delivered me from a lot of things,
you protected me from danger seen and unseen.
You have brought me through a lot of tests and trials,
and I thank you.
I must give you all the honor and praise,
you are worthy to be praised.
Not for what you can do or have done,
its because of who you are.

Like the song says... "There is nobody greater than you."
Lord, I know that my flesh gets weak sometimes,
and you are the deliverer of my temptations.
Lord, through your word it kept me posted
and my mind stayed on you.
I know you woke me up early this morning Lord,
and I thank you.
Whatever it is that you are trying to tell me Lord,
I am ready to receive it.

(Zephaniah 1:7-18)

Lord, what I get out of this is, there will be judgement on the land and wrath will come upon the people because of deceit and violence.

Life Chances

Life gives you several chances to cheat death.
Once life is over, is anything left?
Life gives you a chance to become what you wish.
Don't die, knowing there were things you've missed.
Life gives you a chance to become rich,
and it allows you to become poor.
Life doesn't give you any rules to your decisions.
However, you will learn them after each mission.

Snack Shop

He told me that he had an idea.
As time passed by,
I asked him what the idea was.
He told me that he was going to build a home,
he pointed out a piece of land and told
me that it belonged to his grandfather.
I then remembered his house
on the land.

The house sat next door and
there was a lot going on
and it was considered the hood.
He was a very poor man.
Years passed and the man
built a brick home.
A snack restaurant to-go
is a one-of-a-kind
snack shop that everyone
should see.

I admired this man because

even during Covid he managed
to stay open till this day.
The help and courage that he had
stayed with him and together
it is a beautiful place.

You Are Beautiful...

You are Beautiful

You are beautiful, sexy, and fine.
How would the world be
without you on my mind.
When I look at you,
you give me a thrill.
You've shown love and your good will.

When two women

When two women and one man
were walking down the street,
one woman stopped
and was left behind,
Why?
Because her friend,
was not around.

When Is The Best Time...

When is the best time

When is the best time to think?
What kind of question is that?
Thinking comes along with
the remembrance of the mind.

How can you?

How can you make two into one?
Do two good things one day!

When a light

When a light shines in your mind,
It should also shine in your heart.

I Remember...

I Remember

I remember reading, writing, and arithmetic...
Now its' religion, politics, athletics, and drama.

If loving

If loving people is right,
how about a person
you think isn't bright?

Technology

Technology is moving
at a rapid pace.
Will we take part
in the race?

Can We Live...

Can we live

Can we live Without Poetry-Poems?
No! Poetry-Poems are everyday
Living, acting, and playing the part.

It is smart to

It is smart to do right,
but if you do wrong
it will make you remember.

There Are People...

There are people

There are people that
believe that finance and
Romans will enter paradise.

You are better

You are better in and out.
When are the best times to be in love?
In the morning, noon and at night.
Which ever we choose.
It will be like paradise,
Is that good news?
I think so!
Do you agree?

One Day I Was In A Store

One day I was in a store...
I met a nice lady that everyone should know,
she said, "Hello! How are you doing today?"
My reply was, "Okay."
When you are in the presence of her
you enjoy her and ask her questions.
It seems like she already knows.
Just the idea of speaking with her,
you feel that a good day is headed way.
When you see her, you will know that
the day is about to be good.
When you walk in the door she will
greet you and say, "Hello! How are you today?"

You Know A Neighbor

You know a neighbor is just like a friend,
because they stay in touch whenever they can.
I wonder what they are doing day by day.
I hope there is a window for them to
look out of and I also hope there is a T.V. for them
to look at.
Rather it's looking out the window or looking at the T.V.,
do whatever you choose freely.
Smile and know that your friendly neighbor
may be looking out the window or at the T.V. too.

When A Princess

When a princess lives long, her demeaner is shown.
Everyone knows she was that way all along.
When she lays down, she is beautiful even in her sleep.
A princess is not born everyday,
but she looks at herself in the mirror and
knows she's born that way.

There Is A Woman

There is a woman, she is beautiful and fine!
I love her all the time.
I always ask her, "How are you?"
She always says, "I am great, how are you?"
When she talks, and smiles I feel good inside.
She knows when I write she will enjoy
it day and night.

I Know A Lady

I know a lady, she works in a bank.
How would you know her when you see her?
If you are in line or you are having a seat,
she will let you know how long it will be.
When you walk in the bank,
she will make you feel at home.
Her kindness is like no other.

Lady

There is a lady so beautiful and kind
and she's that way all the time.

Put pride in what you do,
it is a part of you.
The beauty you have in and out,
there is not a doubt.

When she's cooking, baking, cleaning,
and singing at the church, she takes it upon
herself to be a good steward.

Keeping the good work alive!
Take care of yourself.
What a lady and more.

Man

When every man marries...
Every man doesn't marry his wife.
When you marry your wife
you will know it.
Is that a fact?
Leave it like that.

Your Face Is Beautiful

Your face is beautiful.
Your body is fine.
Your body is curvy like a bottle of wine.

You're Special!

I Love You

I love you,
can you tell?
The flowers in the air
always give you a great smell.
I love you in and out.
Never forget to love me,
there is no doubt.

When I See You

When I see you,
I love you more.
I hate when it's time to go.
I know you will see me when you can.
I love and admire you sweetheart all over again.

A Good Neighbor's Love

A good neighbor will love you, as they love themselves.
They will share with you their best
and not what they have left.
They give you something usable and
not what they throw out.
A good neighbor's love, it will last forever.
For a good neighbor that loves everybody,
except to go to heaven, for the bible says to us,
love ye one another.

Love is sharing.
Love is giving.
Love is lending a helping hand.
That's what a good neighbor will do.
They will visit you when you are sick.
They will visit you when you are well.
They will always speak a kind word.
Sometimes they sound like bells.

They will visit you in the morning.
They will visit you at night.
They will do all they can,
to make sure everything is alright.
And when it is done, you won't go wrong.
A good neighbor who loves you,
their love is so strong,
it will last and last forever.
It will go on forever.
Amen.

I Love When You Love Me Baby

I love when you love me.
I don't want your love to hurt me,
I love you very tender.
Tender loving is the way it will be,
Sometimes you say I hurt you baby,
you know I really didn't mean to.
I'm going to keep on working to please you.
I don't want us to always worry.
You know we were born and trained,
You know we was always together,
I'm going to see that it will stay that way.
I love when you love me
I don't want your love to hurt me,
It's time for crying,
a time to tell a lie,
but this is no for time for that.

Let me tell you baby,
you know I always love you.

I can go back to the beginning.
I told you I will take care of you,
You are my pretty baby.
You will always be pretty to me.
I remember on time,
When our love was on the way down.
We stood up together,
and we put all of that behind.

When we are not together,
life just don't seem right.
If I can't have your love,
I'm sure I will die.
I love when you love me.
I don't want your love to hurt me.
Do you understand what I am telling you?
I know,
Oh, oh.
I am so happy and it's all because of you,
I love when you love me.

I Love To See Your Light Shine

I love to see your light shining.
It reminds me of the moon in the sky.
Yes, I love to see your light shining.
If it was not for you baby,
what would I do?
One of the greater things in the world,
is being in love with you.
That pretty blue dress you have on,
will light up everybody's eyes.

I love to see your light shining,
as your light shines on me.
Whenever I see you, you know I want
to be with you.
You know I want to be with you.
So don't ask me no question.
I tell you no lie.
The idea of losing you,
if it was true I would lay down and die.

I love to see your light shining.
It brings out the best in you.
Every time you look at me baby.
Every time you give me a kiss,
even if I don't do the right thing.
You know how much I love you.

You know I loved you all of the time.
Let's not make no mistakes,
because our love will be the best plan.
Let us always keep talking and
let us always be true.
There will always be a place in my heart
for you and that place others may can see.
That's good enough for you, and me.
Don't worry about people trying to ruin your life.
They don't have a vision of our love.
You will stay on their minds.

I love to see your light shine.

The Love Of Christmas

Lady/Man: The love of Christmas. If it wasn't for Jesus, there wouldn't be a Christmas holiday at all. My Jesus' love is a miracle, and this is all we need to know.

Lady: God will never leave you. His love is true. Without God's love, I don't know what I will do.

Lady/Man: Christmas songs are playing. How do you feel? Every time I think about Jesus, he gives me a thrill. The love of Christmas, I wonder what you see. I hope you see angels, watching over you and me.

Man: Jesus is everywhere. We're never alone, because this Christmas will find us at home.

Lady: The love of Christmas, Jesus is always right. If it wasn't for Jesus, he didn't put up a fight.

Man: The love of Christmas, thanks to you my Lord. Everything came true.

Lady/Man: Merry Christmas, and truly, a Happy New Year.

Hello Weekend

Good-bye pain.
I love to see the weekend come because
I know my baby will be back again.
The days are so long and the nights are so sad.
I know when my baby comes back again
she will make me glad.
Weekends, oh I hate to see you go.
The weekdays can be so lonely sometimes.
I don't think they are coming back any more.
I wonder if she loves me, or if she is just playing a game.
Sometimes I am dangling like a puppet on a string.
I love you my baby.
Baby, it may not show the way I love you.
I guess you will never know.
Weekends, oh, hurry and come back again.
It is so hard waiting sometimes.
I cannot stand the pain.
If you treat me good and be truthful, you
will never have to worry about me hurting you.
Love and happiness, that is what we will have.
Our love will never be spread between

nobody but me and you,
Weekends, weekends have come and gone.
I don't feel so lonely.
My baby's love keeps me holding on.
I need your love so bad.
If I thought this was a one sided love,
oh I would be so sad.
Hello weekends.

www.ingramcontent.com/pod-product-compliance
Lightning Source LLC
Chambersburg PA
CBHW030557080526
44585CB00012B/413